DRAWINGS OF SIR EDWARD BURNE-JONES

DRAWINGS OF THE

GREAT MASTERS

STUDY IN RED CHALK

DRAWINGS OF SIR EDWARD BURNE-JONES

LONDON. GEORGE NEWNES LIMITED
SOUTHAMPTON STREET. STRAND. w.c.
NEW YORK. CHARLES SCRIBNER'S SONS

LIST OF ILLUSTRATIONS

LIST OF ILLUSTRATIONS—*continued*

THE DRAWINGS OF SIR E. BURNE-JONES
BY T. MARTIN WOOD

IN the case of an art so personal to himself as was the latter work of Burne-Jones when the influence of Rossetti had faded, criticism finds itself ranged either with those who love or those who hate its mournful romanticism. Admiration will, however, never be withheld the perfect expression the painter was able to achieve within the vocabulary of his limited technique. Throughout his work a fire of conception is traceable that does not wane even in the slightest or the most matter of fact of his studies, and no painter perhaps has possessed in such a marked degree the power of infusing his sketches with so much of the meaning and of the spirit that haunt his finished paintings. In building up a picture, snowball fashion, each succeeding study seemed to bring him nearer and nearer to that harmony in design of which he was such an undoubted master. For the pedantry of his methods Ruskin may to some extent be blamed or praised. In drawing Burne-Jones never admitted *suggestion*, the term artists use for a result reached as it were by illusion. To be able to suggest what is there without carrying the pencil laboriously into detail in search of outline is part of the knowledge and certainty of an artist's achievement which bespeak a master. The great draughtsmen have always, as they gained in power, gradually relinquished their tight hold upon outline for this subtler and truer observation. However, it has generally been that, working within a narrow boundary, consciously restricted or outwardly controlled, artists have arrived at their happiest results, and so we find that often it is in his drawings that Burne-Jones reaches his highest perfection of beauty.

Of the drawings of painters none afford so complete an index to the stages of their technical advancement as do those of Burne-Jones. The at first stiff archaic drapery became more suave in its lines as it grew easier for him to render the variety of shapes taken by an impressionable substance, and a lithe activity gradually took the place of the primitive figure-drawing in his earlier subjects. As he advanced he grew less fond of simplicity and more

I

fond of multitudinous folds, crowded imagery, and complexity of design, reversing in this the line along which most painters have developed, that is to say, towards a greater simplicity and breadth of handling. It is easy to understand the fascination that, with his increasing powers, he found in drawing over and over again things which before had presented so much difficulty, but it is just this lack of repose in the painter's work, coupled with an enthusiasm for design which spent itself in never-ending detail, that proves such a constant source of irritation to some of his critics. The pleasure he took in filling up his spaces with decoration wherever opportunity occurred was largely the outcome of his unlimited invention. This inventiveness made him marvellously independent in his art; his figures are not placed in historical surroundings, all the accessories and all the figures are dominated by his imagination, and in his imaginings there is none of the vagueness, say of Blake, for his art was never one of abstractions. He delighted as keenly as any of the Dutch painters in the beauty of the surfaces and the shapes of visible things. His extravagant invention received its stimulus always from this delight. It is this realism that makes him able to convey so clearly to other minds the atmosphere in which his own was living, for his transcendentalism was of a kind that found true expression only through the medium of tangible things. Perhaps it is for this reason that he was able to invest his studies with so much of the meaning of his completed paintings, for it is in his studies that we are most aware of that sustained sympathy of observation that made him Pre-Raphaelite less by theory than by instinct.

He is able to convey to us some of the sheer pleasure he found in such things as the folded petals of flowers and the embroidery on robes and dresses. The great love he had for flowers, his admiration for the maiden-like grace of some and the complex leaves of others, did not allow him to find satisfaction in treating them as notes of colour only. And this exactness and care which gave him such pleasure in drawing the outstretched wing of a bird and tracing with map-like accuracy its vivid or its fading pattern never degenerated into uninspired labour. Often these studies ended abruptly, some-times possibly for the sake of emphasis, but in most cases owing to a feeling that he had extracted what he was in search of, and the protraction of the minute study would no longer give him pleasure. His drawing never reached that point at which his fingers, ceasing to answer to nervous inspiration, would descend to mechanical delineation. For this reason his drawings keep a tender grey, gaining stability only from the added pressure on the pencil here and there, but never anywhere is more of blackness or strength apparent than could readily be given in the instinctive pressure of the hand following the dictation of fine feeling. Just in this, for a moment, perhaps, his art touches hands with work so antagonistic in spirit as the work of Whistler. But it quickly parts company, for Whistler by his genius as a painter carried the inspiration of touch throughout his largest paintings.

It is difficult to know exactly what place the paintings of Burne-Jones would hold judged merely from the standpoint of paint considered for its own sake. But the ardent and extraordinary temperament that shows itself in their strange pageantry makes it impossible to consider them with mind detached from their overwhelming meaning. The art of his great contemporary, who was of such an opposite school, owes its unchallenged place by reason of the perfection of style and the beauty of vision that it evinces. On the other hand Burne-Jones's art is lifted to its high plane by the emotion that so restlessly seeks expression, leading him in his lifetime to such prolonged study for the improvement of his technique. And here we have not so much the disparaged literary motive as a really artistic one, seeing that the artist found paint and pencil only gave him the true means for expression. It is quite possible that had Burne-Jones been able to do things with greater ease we should have missed the careful reverence that is so characteristic of his drawings. Satisfied with the delights of technical accomplishment, too great ease of workmanship breeds in an artist mere exultation in its display. Burne-Jones's tender and beautiful visual power, though it may have suffered from incomplete expression, may, on the other hand, owe much to the very difficulties which, making him less readily satisfied, carried him to greater heights. It is to his powers of self-criticism that we owe the long series of his pencil studies, and it is not unlikely that posterity will come to set more value on them, especially some of the beautifully drawn heads of women, so expressive of his art's intention, than upon his finished paintings, for in no other work of our time is there so much tenderness and delicacy of execution bearing such an intimate message.

There were two periods in the life of the Burne-Jones woman as we know her in his pencil drawings. There was the earlier maiden face, with its rounded form and ingenuousness of expression, and the later period with its added fragility, in which the full Rossetti lips are never seen. Though his lady of this time seems to have grown a little older, she is not quite so sad, and about her lips

3

there clings an added sweetness and her eyes are far less dreamy than they were before. This change is perhaps more noticeable in his drawings than in his paintings—where always his figures seem to fall under the same spell of listless desire. This is probably a little due to the fact, already dwelt upon, that Burne-Jones never attained the same mastery with the brush that he did with the pencil. In all his canvases there is to be seen an imperfect understanding of what painting might become, and he seems in his drawings of faces to get more charm and expression than he can carry into them with paint. Though we are condemned to know his paintings chiefly through reproductions, in one sense we have him in these at his best, for here his curious method of laying on colour ceases to leave on his faces the evidence of what was amateurish in his art.

The way he braided the hair of his women across their fore-heads, or left it floating, was not arrived at by happy accident; there is evidence that its pleasant disposition was the result of much thought. "Taste" is a word which has lost its full meaning through occurring so frequently in the small change of conversation. But taste—that fine perception, so characteristic of the Japanese as a nation—is just what Burne-Jones had in these matters in a super-lative degree. Its possession enabled him in his compositions to arrange flowers and place objects exactly where they should be. Instinctively he varied the binding of the hair and the folds of the robes in figures side by side in a drawing. Here he would tie their draperies with a single girdle, and there with two, one below the other, or he would cross their breasts with closely fitting bands, thus giving variant notes in the harmony of his compositions. Though he may draw a large group of maidens all with the same ecstasy of love-sickness in their faces, there is no sameness in their sad expressions, and though all their movements are restrained within a circle of listless grace, as though upon themselves they imposed a quaint convention, there is a sense of movement always in their action. A very beautiful example of this is the drawing, "Courtesy and Frankness," reproduced among our illustrations. The coquetry that enters into the drapery of Frankness is very charming; it enters into her action and her hair, and there is a spontaneity about her that we could wish to find more often, for she retains all the best characteristics of her sisters, with something added of lightness and grace that we seek for again in vain.

Burne-Jones delighted in a multiplicity of lines relieved by little empty spaces, and the draperies he drew are always crumpled and then smoothed out and crumpled again in order to give him the drawing

4

he wanted, independent of whether in the actual moving of the limbs the folds would come together in that or some quite other way. His arrangement of drapery is always beautiful, and he owes less to the Parthenon than to his own fancy for the rhythm of the folds. This love of folded garments has been pointed out to be characteristic of English painting, and it has been attributed to the fact that we have before us always in our museums all that is best that has come to our age from Athens. To stay where Leighton and Albert Moore left their exercises in this classicism did not please Burne-Jones; he must embroider and colour from east or west all the manner of robes worn by his people, whatever the age in which they are supposed to move. With less of scholarship and more of beauty than his two contemporaries, he sees the Grecian goddesses as he saw the Blessed Lady, not of any one particular time. In this subordination of everything to the emotion of the moment he achieves greatness; had he paused to strip the embroidery of late hands from robes of an older day, or gone back upon his studies to correct this and that detail for the sake of a date, his art would have been less great in proportion as he sacrificed his first conceptions in an attempt to reconcile them with exact scholarship.

Although a Greek feeling for drapery is apparent throughout the work of Burne-Jones, in his drawings of the nude he reverses all their laws of beauty, for he seeks the beauty of the body that clothes the ardent modern soul. Whilst serenity is the keynote of the nude in classic art, in the art of Burne-Jones there is shown traces of that contempt of the soul for the body which animated mediæval Christianity, and is the extreme opposite of that worship of physical beauty which was at once the triumph of the Grecians and the expression of their religion. Burne-Jones is akin to Botticelli in this, but whilst Botticelli's maidens carry with them the impress of an intellectual sadness, the Burne-Jones woman is sad at heart. Less intellectual than those women whose spirit she reincarnates, she has grown less happy with the years, and is more than ever in search of Love, who alone remains, and comes to her over the flowered grass, with the dead leaves of the old gardens clinging to his feet and with wreaths of their roses fading in his hair.

Only the delicate fancy of Burne-Jones's work saves its brooding sadness from being depressing. The traditions which Burne-Jones held in reverence were those which in past times had inspired an art the prototype of his own; he voluntarily bound himself to these traditions, seeing eye to eye with the masters of them, and, for the rest, he might have existed contemporaneously with those masters for all the effect that changing fashions and newly evolving theories in the art of his time had upon him.

The one thing upon which a certain phase of modern art has insisted has been a newer and truer way of seeing nature, our eyes moving rapidly from point to point, our vision only embracing clearly an isolated space with indefiniteness beyond. In this way the impressionist gives us pictures as he sees things, eliminating that which is not embraced in a first vision. In the case of the creative art of Burne-Jones, he did right to work within the conventions he chose and, in not allowing himself to compromise with the methods of imitative art, he preserved throughout his work the essential qualities of a certain school of subjective painting. Yet, though he conveyed to his canvas his subject in all the imaginative atmosphere in which it was conceived, some of his critics have at times adopted an untenable position by finding fault with this consistency, forgetting that only in this way could he exactly achieve his aim.

In his drawings of babies Burne-Jones was delightful, for he alone of modern artists seems to have avoided what may be called the rococo baby—that phenomenon who always seems out of place without an accompanying paraphernalia of music-scrolls and violins. Burne-Jone's babies show the closest observation of baby-life, and there is no more beautiful rendering in art of a baby's unquestioning confidence than the drawing, here illustrated, of the Madonna and Child. His babies play, too, in the clumsy way of real ones and, rarest of qualities, they look as though they could grow to men.

In essaying portraiture with his pencil Burne-Jones was, from his careful method, almost bound to arrive at an accurate delineation of his model, but to copy accurately in this way is but to vie with the camera. Of his ability to infuse everything he touched with the spirit of his genius his portraits give us several remarkable examples. In portraying women he could never quite disentangle his mind from a preconceived type, but as no one ever sees what is not there, we must take it that he had come to look for certain characteristics that affected his imagination in the faces of those he saw about him. He was drawn to certain types and readily discovered in faces any resemblance to his inner vision. The head of Paderewski, as a portrait born of the sympathy between two minds dedicated to beauty, must live amongst great achievements in portraiture. The face of the great pianist too is of the type of Burne-Jones's male faces—the regular and sensitive profile, the eyebrows close to the eyes, the small lips. It is a type *spirituel* rather than spiritual, not rejecting life but caring only for the finest it has to offer.

6

Although Burne-Jones had a long way to make up owing to not starting his art training until most men are well on the road, in one way he had an advantage. It is exceptional that at the outset of his career a painter should find himself upon the path he wishes to tread. He had not to disentangle his art from methods foreign to its aim, and instead of drifting uncertainly round the schools a prey to indecision consequent upon contradictory teaching, he worked from the first under his chosen master. Many serious painters have envied his good fortune in this. That impressionability to what is good in what is alien to their temperament has been the undoing of more than one student, and the long process of assimilating only that which is necessary to themselves from the influences around them, has ended often in pitiful unproductiveness. One cannot say how much the actual technique of Burne-Jones might have gained by the correcting influences of the usual train- ing, but it is permissible to believe that the freedom he enjoyed from the opposition to which such a course would have laid him open, proved, in the case of his peculiar and lonely temperament, wholly to the benefit of his art, as an expression of himself. Rossetti was essentially a teacher—one of those rare beings whose genius was as a cup brimming over. He inspired all those who were attracted to him. A large measure of his own inability to complete his art was due to a nature too full and variable ever to be thoroughly disciplined in the short life at man's disposal. Burne-Jones so far benefited by the example of Rossetti that he resolved to release himself as far as possible by arduous study from the limitations under which he saw the rich genius of his master stifling. Some of his critics have thought that they saw in his early work something they search for in vain later, when good drawing became so much a consideration with him. But if anything was lost in his attempts to transform the character of his work by a stricter observance of form, it was something that was more of Rossetti than of himself. The kinship of sympathy that brought Rossetti and Burne-Jones together was the foundation of one of the most perfect intellectual friendships the world has known. How the sleeping imagination of Burne-Jones was stirred by a chance illustration of Rossetti's that came his way, reads like one of the old tales, in which a chance incident would sometimes reveal to a knight where there lay for him a great adventure.

A sense of the greatness of the task that he had set himself to accomplish, led Burne-Jones to shut himself up, day in and day out, to long hours of uninterrupted work, everything in life being subordinated to the attainment of his artistic purpose. Intensity was the key-note of his whole life and work. He devoted himself to what was his alone to give, and protected the essential part of himself that made for beauty, from what might tend to lessen it in traffic with the world. His refusal to come into contact and make terms with actual existence may have made for narrowness, but it was the narrowness of a perfect garden, shut in by a high wall. From out of the garden flowers might go daily, but no rumour of the world's ugliness was to be brought in.

It is never fatiguing to look at large numbers of Burne-Jones's studies, though, in his endeavour to select nothing short of the best arrangement of form possible, he often drew the same thing many times, merely for the decision of small differences. Some of the charm of his studies lies in the fact that they seem to show that they were made always with great pleasure to himself. His infinite variations on the same theme point to an exuberance of fancy that must have made his real difficulty one only of curbing his invention and his fastidiousness. Altering and embellishing, the supplanting of one perfection by another, might, at the dictation of an extravagant fancy, go on indefinitely, were it not brought to an end by the exercise of self-repression with a certain amount of sacrifice.

The illustrations of this book are arranged for the sake of variety only and not in any accordance with dates of production. In looking through them we are arrested as often by the beauty of the thoughts expressed as by the beauty of the designs. In this we may take for an instance the sketch for "The Entombment" with the strange modernity of its conception of the face of Christ. Here no tradition has been followed, but in what an intimate and reverent way has the artist made this picture, where from the arms of men the Christ is lowered to the grave. The light of the great spirit has not died from the dead face and love still burns under the closed eyes. In the face of the Madonna too, in the drawing for the Church of St. John, Torquay, the same modernity of feeling is apparent, a modernity that makes Burne-Jones as a religious painter perhaps the greatest of his time, for it was his special gift to view such subjects in relation to the feeling of his time, to give to them more than a legendary or historical interest. The Madonna's face is full of that sweet tenderness and refinement of affection that centuries of inherited spiritual experience has given to our English ladies. Over her Son she bends with affection prophetic of what the world was to learn of

8

affection from Him. Her face, as the face of Christ in the picture of the Entombment, in its type stands in romantic relation to our own emotion. Palestine is far away and that story of the East in an old time, but the Madonna by the wayside in the Catholic towns and the Madonna of the Church is here; and that other, still more real Madonna whom men have set up in their hearts to worship as the spirit of all sweet womanhood and whose symbol they have marked as a pure lily against the dark background of their sin. It is because of this intense inner relation to the instinctive religion in man, and to the freedom of his art from empty symbols, that Burne-Jones's religious pictures retain the intimate sentiment which has been sacrificed so often to the conventions of sacred art. His faces have stood for some definite struggle in the soul, some definite act of love. Cold, scholarly symbolism is absent, and what he has drawn is representative of the instinct in man to take a religion from his emotions.

To pass to pictures in which the beauty of his design and the variety of his invention are of paramount interest, the drawings for the story of St. George and the Dragon show, as do many other of his smaller drawings, that something is in them that often ebbed away in the preparations for a large painting. The figure of the priest near the altar in one of the drawings shows too the receptivity of Burne-Jones's imagination to outward impressions, and how he carried those impressions from real life into the life of his art. From some solemn service his memory brought away the impression of the bearing of the standing priest and the slow wreaths of incense ascending. Such drawings as this and the one of " Love and Beauty " would have made famous any artist in black and white; very few painters have been able to make such finished imaginative drawings on a small scale. They are drawn as if they had been Burne-Jones's only business and his only method of expression, and not as though they were done, as was the case, in the intervals from his painting and serious studies for paintings. His dainty imagination had free scope in such drawings and some of them display the most charming qualities of his art.

One quality he always had in a marked degree in his technique; he was able to differentiate between the substance of things and to give to steel a steely surface as he gave to dress its impressionable folds. He was able to give always the particular quality required to indicate surface, turning from the imitation of one thing to another and using the same medium; but, were it one's province to depart from a criticism of his drawings, one might well grumble that he had no care and no reverence for the peculiar qualities of his mediums, for the respective qualities of water-colours, say, or of oils. The dissimilar properties of these mediums, and their different limitations, and the exercising of his art within these limitations apparently held for him no charm. His art loses in this as in that other matter of touch which has already been mentioned. Here, as there, he seemed to enter into a more sensitive understanding of art with his pencil than in the case of his painting. It has been the fashion recently for certain critics in their distaste for the methods of Burne-Jones's painting, to forget his very definite achievements as a draughtsman. It may safely be said of his drawing of a baby, included amongst the illustrations, that such quality of draughtsmanship as is exhibited there, and in many others of his drawings, places him on a level even with those modern masters with the point who have striven after virtuosity alone. The drawing referred to displays the extreme sensitiveness of handling that is modern, and it has besides that which is peculiarly Burne-Jones's own, namely, a beauty which is not wholly of form but was imparted to his work from his own rare nature and which gives that lovable quality to his drawings of certain lovable things.

The study for the face of Lancelot provides us with evidence of just where the genius of Burne-Jones, apart from craftsmanship, was limited; it shows the confines of his imagination, which was not of a dramatic order. Himself concerned with an inward life, the people of his art look in upon themselves; the thoughts and passions that their faces betray are of the soul's own making, not of the tragedy where outward things break in. Into the frowning face of the knight he does not seem to have been able to get the same sincerity of feeling in his drawing as he attains in faces where love as a sweet and not an ugly sorrow holds sway. He sought here to step outside the experiences of his mind to something which must have been imaginary to him, for whom so much that is imaginary to other people was so beautifully real.

Living in a land of make-believe, he pretended things had happened as he painted them, even as children pretend. Painter never lived more in a fairyland of his own making than Burne-Jones, yet a curious reality enters into the strangest of his conceptions. He sets his Madonna and her Child as it were on a throne in a manger overgrown with roses, hardly less a summer-house than a manger, and we do not challenge the veracity of the things he has thus depicted. The air of reality he carried into everything convinces us, we accept these things and they seem so

10

true because whether it be the branches that support the shed, or the flowers and nodding grass that make a carpet for Our Lady, everything is drawn with a realism that would cheat us by its seeming appearance of " every-day." Never attempting subterfuge in vagueness, or escaping a difficulty in indefiniteness of form, everything in his art is as clear and precise as he was clear in his own mind as to how he wished to view these things. From the realism he wedded with his fantasy springs his unusual power of making history an illusory thing, and so it is we feel that in whatever remote place and in however strange a way he has depicted them these things happened so in an older time.

ILLUSTRATIONS

PLATE I

STUDY FOR "THE BRIAR ROSE"

PLATE II

STUDY FOR "THE CAR OF LOVE"

PLATE III

PHOTO HOLLYER

STUDY FOR "THE DREAM"

PLATE IV

PHOTO HOLLYER

COURTESY AND FRANKNESS—ROMANCE OF THE ROSE

PLATE V

ILLUSTRATION FOR "THE ÆNEID"

PLATE VII

ILLUSTRATION FOR "THE ÆNEID"

PLATE IX

ILLUSTRATION FOR "THE ÆNEID"

PLATE X

ILLUSTRATION FOR "THE ÆNEID"

PLATE XI

ILLUSTRATION FOR "THE ÆNEID"

PLATE XII

ILLUSTRATION FOR "THE ÆNEID"

PLATE XIII

ST. GEORGE AND THE DRAGON

PLATE XIV

STUDY FOR "THE CAR OF LOVE"

PLATE XV

ST. GEORGE AND THE DRAGON

PLATE XVI

STUDY FOR "THE SIRENS"

PLATE XVII

STUDY

PLATE XVIII

"THE NATIVITY," ST. JOHN'S, TORQUAY—FRAGMENT

PLATE XIX

THE ENTOMBMENT

PLATE XX

PHOTO HOLLYER

STUDY

PLATE XXI

STUDY FOR LANCELOT

PLATE XXII

EB-J
1893
Study for LAMORAK
one seated on the
ROUND TABLE
for the Tapestry of the
MORTE D'ARTHVR

PHOTO HOLLYER

STUDY FOR LAMORAK

PLATE XXIII

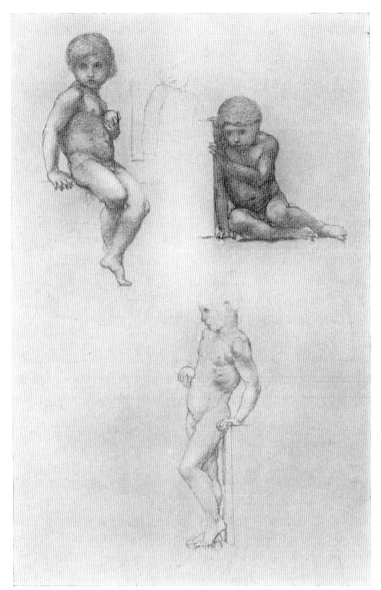

PHOTO HOLLYER

STUDIES OF CHILDREN

PLATE XXIV

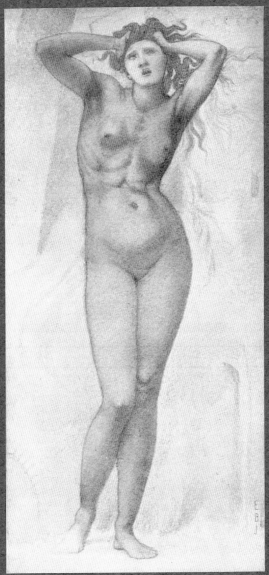

LIFE STUDY

PHOTO HOLLYER

PLATE XXV

GAWAIN

EBJ
1893
study for the
REJECTION OF·
GAWAIN μ C.
Taylor F ... in the MORTE D'ARTHVR.

PHOTO HOLLYER

STUDY FOR GAWAIN

PLATE XXVI

EB-J
1893·
Study for the
arming of the
Knight in
the Legend of
the MORTE
D'ARTHUR

STUDY

PLATE XXVII

PHOTO HOLLYER

STUDIES OF ARMOUR

PLATE XXVIII

PORTRAIT STUDY

PLATE XXIX

STUDY FOR "THE MASQUE OF CUPID"

PLATE XXX

STUDY FOR "THE MASQUE OF CUPID"

PLATE XXXI

STUDY FOR "THE MASQUE OF CUPID"

PLATE XXXII

PHOTO HOLLYER

"ASGARD"
DESIGN FOR WINDOW

PLATE XXXIII

PHOTO HOLLYER

" THOR "
DESIGN FOR WINDOW

PLATE XXXIV

PHOTO HOLLYER

"FREY"
DESIGN FOR WINDOW

PLATE XXXV

LOVE AND BEAUTY—ROMANCE OF THE ROSE

PLATE XXXVI

FIGHTING BOYS

PLATE XXXVII

SUMMER   WINTER

PLATE XXXVIII

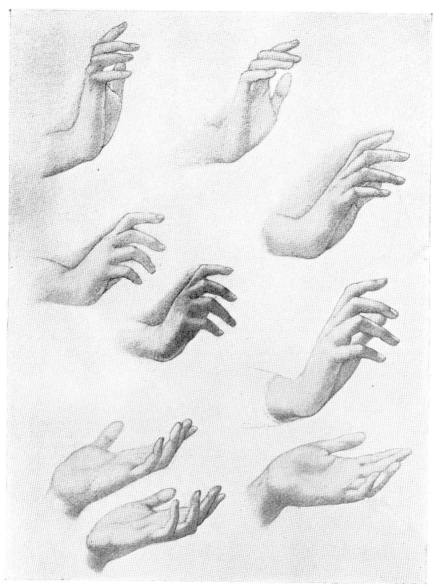

STUDIES OF HANDS

PLATE XXXIX

PHOTO HOLLYER

FIGHTING CATS

PLATE XL

STUDIES FOR "THE GOLDEN STAIRS"

PLATE XLI

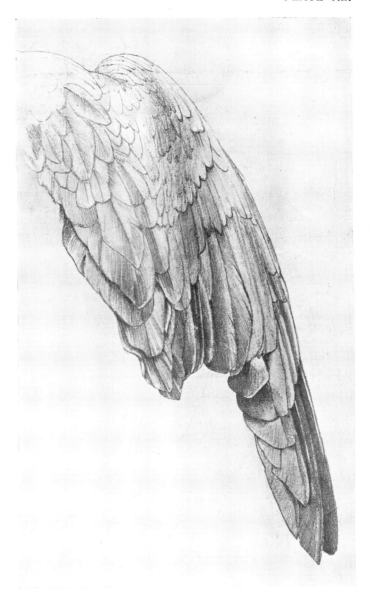

STUDY OF A WING

PLATE XLII

STUDY ON BROWN PAPER

PLATE XLV

PADEREWSKI

PLATE XLVI

CASSANDRA